CHINA IN TRANSITION

EMERGING MARKETS: REFORM AND DEVELOPMENT IN CHINA

China in Transition

Additional books in this series can be found on Nova's website under the Series tab.

Additional E-books in this series can be found on Nova's website under the E-book tab.

CHINA IN TRANSITION

EMERGING MARKETS: REFORM AND DEVELOPMENT IN CHINA

LI XIAOXI
LIN YONGSHENG
AND
LIU YIMENG

Novinka
Nova Science Publishers, Inc.
New York

For permission to use material from this book please contact us:
Telephone 631-231-7269; Fax 631-231-8175
Web Site: http://www.novapublishers.com

LIBRARY OF CONGRESS CATALOGING-IN-PUBLICATION DATA

Available upon Request
ISBN: 978-1-61668-769-4

Published by Nova Science Publishers, Inc. † New York

CONTENTS

PREFACE

On Sept. 4, 2009, the finance ministers and central bank presidents of China, India, Brazil and Russia, known as the BRICs, had a conference in London. Issues about the present global financial situation, the countermeasures by the four countries against the crisis, the agenda at the third G-20 summit and the reform of global financial institutions etc. were discussed and a consensus reached. The Chinese delegates led by Xie Xuren, Finance Minister of China, and Yi Gang, Vice President of the People's Bank of China attended the conference. Also present were Kudrin, Mantega and Mukherjee, Finance Minister of Russia, Brazil and India respectively. It was stated at the meeting that the global economy was recovering thanks to the financial rescue and stimulus plans taken worldwide and that the emerging economies played an important role therein. The financial ministers and central bank presidents of the BRICs issued a united communiqué at the conference[1].

Let's discuss how the term BRICs came into being and its connection with the emerging economies.

It dated back to 1994 when the concept of emerging markets was introduced in the *National Export Strategy* of the U.S. Department of Commerce: " Perhaps the most promising opportunities for U.S. firms in the next several decades can be found in the Big Emerging Markets (BEMs)...10 markets which are expected to account for over 40 percent of total global imports (excluding intra-EU trade) over the next 20 years. The BEMs are: Mexico, Argentina, Brazil, the Chinese Economic Area, India, Indonesia,

---

[1] Source: Xinhua News Agency, London Branch, Sep.4, 2009.

South Korea, Poland, Turkey, and South Africa.". Then a policy of big emerging markets was formulated[2].

IMF divided the world into two categories[3]: the advanced economy including U.S., Eurozone (inc. Germany, France, Italy and Spain), Japan, U.K., Canada, other advanced economies and the emerging industrial countries of Asia; the emerging and developing economy including Africa (inc. Sub-Sahara Africa), Central Europe and Eastern Europe, CIS (Russia and the other member states), the developing countries of Asia (China, India), ASEAN (Indonesia, Malaysia, Philippine, Thailand, Vietnam), Middle East, Brazil and Mexico. The share of GDP contributed by the emerging markets (inc. the emerging industrial countries of Asia, the emerging markets worldwide and the developing countries) to the world has increased from 23.56% in 1990 to 33.31%[4] in 2008, changing the global economic territory significantly.

The BRICs and VISTA are outstanding among the emerging markets. The term BRICs comes form the initials of Brazil, Russia, India and China respectively. The BRICs account for 26% of the world territory and 42% of the world population. From 2006 to 2008, the BRICs have an average economic growth of 10.7%[5]. Their international influence grows with their rapid economic development. Brazil is called the world material base, Russia the gas station of the world, India the office of the world and China the factory of the world.

Jim O'Neill, the chief economist of Goldman Sachs, first introduced the term BRICs in *The World Needs Better Economic BRICs* in November 2001. The BRICs did not attract the world attention until Goldman Sachs released a report *Dreaming with BRICs* on October 1st 2003. According to the report, the GDP of BRICs will exceed that of the six industrial countries and the value of its stock market will grow by 66 times in 50 years. It will have a stock market three times greater and a middle class of 800 million people in 10 years, which exceeds that of U.S., Western Europe and Japan combined. The report predicts

---

[2] Department of Commerce (2004). *National Export Strategy: the second annual report of the Trade Promotion Coordinating Committee.* http://www.archive.org/details/nationalexportst00unit.

[3] IMF (2004). *World Economic Outlook: Advancing Structural Reforms.* http://www.imf.org/external/ pubs/ft/weo/2004/01/.

[4] Source: Calculated according to data of World Economic Outlook Database of IMF, April 2009. http://www.imf.org/external/pubs/ft/weo/2009/01/weodata/index.aspx.

[5] Source: Xinhua News Agency. Also see http://news.xinhuanet.com/world/2009-04/02/ content_11116584.htm.

that the BRICs will lead the energy, natural resources and capital markets and become the most important consumption market of the world[6].

On December 2005, Goldman Sachs introduced the term Next-11 (N-11 for short) for 11 emerging markets whose economic potential is next to the BRICs. Those markets are Mexico, Indonesia, Nigeria, Korea, Vietnam, Turkey, Philippines, Egypt, Pakistan, Iran and Bangladesh. According to Goldman Sachs, the GDP of the BRICs and N-11 accounted for only a quarter of G7 in 2005 but will exceed the latter in 2035. The GDP of the N-11 will grow by 11 times in 2050, being equivalent of U.S. or four times as great as Japan[7].

In 2007, Akashi Kadokura, chief of Institute of Japan for BRICs, introduced the concept of VISTA for the most promising emerging markets next to the BRICs. The term VISTA comes from the initials of Vietnam, Indonesia, South Africa, Turkey and Argentina[8]. The nine economies of BRICs and VISTAs have become the most active economy of the world.

The above-mentioned countries are recognized worldwide as the emerging economies because they all have the institution of market economy and sustain a rapid economic growth.

Next, we will analyze China, an emerging market and one of the BRICs, in terms of its positioning as an emerging market, its experience in shifting from planned economy to market economy, its practice in handling the global financial crisis and its new roles in international economy etc.

---

[6] Goldman Sachs (October 2003). Global Economics Paper No.99, *Dreaming with BRICs: The Path to 2050.*

[7] Goldman Sachs (March 2007). Global Economics Paper No: 153: *The N-11: More Than an Acronym.*

[8] Akashi Kadokura (2007). *VISTA: Countries with New Potentials.* Financial View, 2007 (12).

Chapter 1

POSITIONING: AN EMERGING MARKET

It is commonly believed that China is an emerging market. To illustrate it, we need to explain that China is emerging as a new star in the world economy as well as that China is a market economy instead of a planned economy. We will dicuss from the following three dimensions in this part: the role of emerging markets in the global economy, China's impact on the world supply and demand and China's role as a developing market economy.

1.1. THE ROLE OF THE EMERGING MARKETS IN GLOBAL ECONOMY

The emerging markets boast rapid economic growth and make greater contributions to the global economic growth.

Table 1. Contribution of Major Countries and Regions to World GDP(unit:%)

Year	USA	Japan	Germany	G7	9 Emerging markets	Brics	China	Brazil	Russia	India
2000	31.1	14.8	6	66.5	10.7	8.2	3.8	2.1	0.8	1.5
2007	25.2	8	6.1	55.3	15.8	12.7	5.8	2.4	2.4	2.2
2008	23.6	8.2	6.1	53.2	17.1	13.8	6.4	2.7	2.7	2.0

Source: Calculated with reference of the data from World Bank DDP database and World Development Indicators Database.

Firstly, The Emerging Markets Slow Down the Plunge of the Global Economy, Stabilizing the Economic Fluctuation

During the international financial crisis, although the emerging markets are also experiencing a downslide economy, their decline was generally less than the developed economies. For instance, in the fourth quarter of 2008, the GDP growth of the developed countries was almost all minus: U. S. -0.8%, Eurozone -1.7%, UK -1.8%, Japan -4.4%, etc., while that of the emerging markets hit 3.63%: Russia 1.1%, Brazil 1.3%, India 4.8%, China 6.8%, etc. With the emerging markets sustaining an economic growth against a global recession, the severe recession of the developed countries was mitigated and the world average output was able to keep a growth of 0.2% in the same period[1].

The reason that the emerging markets helped against the downturn of the global economy lies in their sustainable economic growth, and, more importantly, their growing share in the global economic aggregate (see Table 1).

The table shows that the share of the total GDP of the emerging markets (Brazil, Russia, China, Vietnam, India, South Africa, Turkey, Argentina)in the world GDP has increased from 10.7% in 2000 to 17.1% in 2008 , while that of the seven western countries (USA, Japan, Germany, France, UK, Italy, Canada)in the same period dropped from 66.5% to 53.2%. According to the GDP ranking list released by the World Bank[2], the BRICs' GDP amounted to US $8.3 trillion in 2008, in which the GDP of China accounted for 46.5% by US $3.86 trillion, Russia and Brazil for 19.4% by US $ 1.61 trillion each, and India came last with 14.7% by US $1.22 trillion. Furthermore, the BRICs have all ascended in the GDP world ranking and become the top twelve GDP contributors in the world. It has been recognized that the emerging markets play a role as an economic stabilizer during the severe global economic fluctuation.

---

[1] Data source: Calculated with reference of the data from *World Economic Outlook Database*, IMF, April 2009.

[2] Data source: Calculated with the reference of the data of *World Development Indicators Database*, World Bank.

Secondly, the Emerging Markets Promote the Global Economic Development

The emerging markets promote the global economic growth while developing their own economy. Take the BRICs. The BRICs have become the outstanding ones of the emerging markets because they are sustaining a rapid growth and enjoying increasingly stronger economic strength in past few years. The real growth rates of the BRICs are much higher than other countries in 2008. China boasts the highest growth of 9.0%, followed by India of 7.3%, Russia of 5.6% and Brazil of 5.1%. The average growth of the BRICs is 10.7% from 2006 to 2008 according to data from IMF[3]. Goldman Sachs' latest forecast indicates that the global economy will suffer a contraction of 1.1% this year, while the BRICs will still grow by 4.8% and the global economy will increase by 3.3% next year, while the BRICs will probably enjoy a growth of 8.8%.[4]

As the economic drivers, the emerging markets accounted for 50% of the world GDP, 40% of the world trade volume and 70% of the world foreign exchange reserve in 2008, in which China, Russia and India all hold significant amount of foreign exchange reserves. Together with China, Indian has also become the world's most attractive investment location next to U.S. by a growth of 6%-7% for more than ten years. With an annual average growth of 7.8% over the past 8 years, Russia has become one of the top ten economies again. The economic growth of Brazil has been 4%-5% in recent years. The contribution of the BRICs to the global economy growth in 2008 exceeded 50%.[5]

The emerging markets are boosting the global trade by their strong consumption capacity, The U.S. consumption market has been indispensable to the global consumption market all the time but now it is time to stress the role of the emerging markets in the growth of the global consumption demand. Since the outbreak of the global financial crisis, with the U.S. consumption being sluggish, the emerging markets have become a major impetus to the expansion of the global consumption market by a total of population accounting for over 50% of the world and a rising middle class. The high-end

---

[3] Data source: Calculated with the reference of the data of *World Economic Outlook Database*, IMF, April 2009.

[4] Shang Jun, Fu Yunwei. *Emerging markets step onto historical front on response to financial crisis. Ecnomic Information Daily*, Sep. 16th, 2009.

[5] Data source: Xinhua News Agency. http://news.xinhuanet.com/world/2009-04/02/content_11116584.htm

firms of the developed countries are busy transferring product lines to the emerging markets in recent years for the much cheaper labor force but more importantly the strong absorbing capacity there. Since the beginning of this year, China has been sending quite a few trade and investment promotion delegations to Europe, U.S. and the member countries of the Shanghai Cooperation Organization to bolster the trade and investment for the Chinese and foreign firms hit by the crisis, which also promoted the economic development of these countries to some extent.

Thirdly, the Emerging Markets Accelerate the Global Technological Progress and Industry Upgrading

International competitive capacity is an aggregate indicator and reflects a country's progress on many aspects, including the breakthrough in technological progress and industry upgrading. *The Global Competitiveness Report 2009-2010* (hereinafter referred to as *Report*) announced by World Economic Forum indicates that in the chosen 132 economies China's competitiveness ranking ascended to the 29th from the 28th, topping the other BRICs. The ranking of India and Brazil also ascended. The World Economic Forum holds that the global competitiveness indicator is determined by the infrastructure, efficiency, innovation and maturity which break down again to 12 items. According to its yearly *The Global Competitiveness Report*[6] which is an aggregate evaluation of a country, there has been considerable upgrade of the emerging markets' international competitiveness, which shows that their technological progress is contributing more and more to the global technological progress.

The four countries of the BRICs focus on different aspects of economy and enjoy different strengths. China's manufacturing industry, Russia's energy industry, Brazil's mining industry and India's information technology industry are the pillar industry of each and have a strong competitive edge in the world. Facing the new world economic environment, the BRICs' dynamic growth lay a solid foundation for intensifying the advantages of their technology and industry. For instance, China's industry promotion program and RMB 4 trillion economic stimulus plan will lead to another round of industrial upgrading with still huge potential in the infant industries including new

---

[6] Data source: Xinhua News Agency. http://news.xinhuanet.com/fortune/2009-09/08/content_12016501.htm

energy industry, environmental protection industry, biomedicine industry and electronic information industry, etc. China is taking the lead in the economic recovery, which is crucial to the full recovery of the world economy and is conducive to forming a new world economic growth point.

Fourthly, the Emerging Markets Boost Global Economic Cooperation

The boosting is through stronger cooperation between the emerging markets themselves and between the emerging markets and the developed countries.

There are many examples about the reinforcement of the cooperation among the emerging markets. Here, we will only take the BRICs as an example. With complementary advantages with each other, the BRICs boast tremendous potential for collaboration. On behalf of the emerging markets, the BRICs are intensifying dialogues and cooperation with each other, and jointly claiming for the interests for the developing countries. With more exchanges being made between the leaders, the BRICs have become a major power in responding to the global financial crisis. The BRICs play an important role in the joint fight around the world against the global financial crisis, coordinating to reform the international financial system, making propositions in favor of the developing countries, making promotions in strengthening international financial regulation, reforming the international financial organizations, and so on.

The emerging markets strengthen the ties with the developed countries and seek mutual development by promoting the trade and investment liberalization, energy saving and environmental protection and new energy development. Globally, the emerging markets hold North-South dialogues with the developed countries in a positive and constructive manner. The dialogue between G-20, G-8 and the developing countries has become an important platform for the major developing countries and developed countries to meet, coordinate and cooperate. During the world's joint fight against the global financial crisis, the emerging economies play the leading role and receive considerable attention for their rising international status and the increasingly active role in international activities. They actively advocate and protect the interests of the developing countries in the reform of international financial system, make significant contributions to creating a fair, equitable, inclusive and well-organized financial order and to establishing a healthy system for the development of the global economy.

1.2. CHINA: AN INFLUENCER OF THE WORLD MARKET[7]

An important feature of emerging markets is their growing impact on the world market, which enables them to take a new role in the international stage. China is just one of them.

Firstly, China Takes a Significant Share in the Commodity Export Market of the World

In 1950, China only ranked the 27th in the world in aggregate export, and remained the same rank within almost 30 years until with one rank higher in 1980. Thereafter, it has been ascending rapidly in the rank: 15th in 1990, 6th in 2001, 3rd from 2004 to 2006, and finally the second in 2007 and 2008.

Aggregate export of China has increased by 146 times during 1979-2008, from US $ 9.75 billion in 1978 to US $ 1.43 trillion in 2008, with an annual average growth of 18.1%. By 2008, the export of China accounts for 8.9% of the world total export.

More than 210 categories of China's industrial products rank first in the world. According to the data from the Ministry of Industry and Information Technology of China, export of the light industry products accounts for 20% of China's total export, among which many products take up more than half of the world market shares, such as household electric appliances, leather, furniture, feather products, ceramic, bicycle, and so on. In addition, China is a predominant producer and exporter of rare earth products in the world.

Recent data from WTO show that, although China's commodity export decreased by 21.7% in the first half of 2009 year on year, China has outpaced Germany and become the biggest commodity exporter in the world by an export of US $521.7 billion. Certainly, it must be noted that more than half of China's export in 2008 was created by the foreign funded firms.

---

[7] Unless otherwise stated, data in this section are from a report by China's National Bureau of Statistics. See http://www.stats.gov.cn/tjfx/ztfx/qzxzgcl60zn/index.htm

Secondly, China Becomes an Increasingly Important Commodity Importer in the World

The aggregate import of China has increased by 103 times during 1979-2008, from US $ 10.89 billion to US $ 1.13 trillion, with an annual average growth of 16.7%. By 2008, the import of China accounts for 6.9% of the world aggregate imports. In the first half of 2009, with a decline of 25.4% year on year, China's import still amounts to US $424.54 billion.

Based on international experiences, a country's consumption go up rapidly when its GDP per capita exceeds US $2,000. China's big population possesses enormous potential in purchasing power. With an annual average growth of 13.1% during the past five years, the consumption in China has the potential to be further promoted. It is estimated that by 2014, China will be the biggest market for luxuries, accounting for 23% of the world aggregate. The expenditure on international travel has increased from US $3.7 billion in 1995 to US $33.3 billion in 2007 in China, with a share up from 0.8% to 3.6% of the world aggregate. Furthermore, the rural consumption in China is still fairly low, which is expected to be improved significantly, with the urban- rural gap being reduced gradually.

In particular, overseas group purchase is often promoted by Chinese government. For example, during Premier Wen's visit to Europe around the end of January and beginning of February in 2009, 38 cooperative agreements were signed between China and the EU as well as the four European countries, amounting to RMB 15 billion and covering multiple fields including financial, information technology, logistics, aviation, energy, telecommunication, etc. Since the end of February, the Chinese purchasing delegation has been to Europe to put the agreements into effects. The delegation is consisted of both government officials as well as the people from multiple business lines such as energy, medicine, service, light industry, machine and electrical products, textiles, and so on, and signed the detailed purchase contracts on fields stated above.[8]

---

[8] Source: http://www.chinanews.com.cn.

Thirdly, China's Service Trade Share in the World Also Grows Rapidly

In 2008, the aggregate service trade of China has increased to US $ 304.5 billion from US $ 4.4 billion in 1982, with a share of China's total foreign trade up to 10.6% from 9.4%. The share of China's service trade in that of the world has also increased from 0.6% in 1982 to 4.2% in 2008, up from 34th to 5th in rank. During 1983-2008, China's service trade had an annual average growth of 17.7%, 8.7 % higher than the world service trade growth in the same period, and grew by 21.3% in 2008, by 10.3% higher than that of the world (11.0%).[9]

Fourthly, China Participates Actively in International Project Contracting Market

The contract amount of China's international project contracting has increased from US $ 33 million in 1979 to US $ 104.6 billion in 2008, among which the completed turnover has increased to US $ 56.6 billion from US $ 1.48 billion. It was under the background of the rapid growth of China's international economic cooperation that these achievements were obtained. In 1979, only 36 contracts were signed for international economic cooperation. This figure hit 3,100 in 1989 and 164,000 by 2008, and the contract amount increased from US $50 million in 1979 to US $ 2.21 billion in 1989 and US $113 billion in 2008.

China has a strong team engaged in international economic cooperation, consisting of more than 1,000 firms with a complete range of business lines and excellent international competitiveness. In 2007, 49 Chinese firms appeared in the list of world Top 225 Contractors in the U.S. *Engineering News Record* (ENR) , 14 of which were in the list of top 100 contractors.

Last, China's Supply and Demand Has a Significant Impact on World Investing Market

Through introducing foreign investments and promoting overseas direct investment (ODI), China has greatly enhanced its comprehensive

---

9 Source: website of the Department of Commerce.

competitiveness and also has a significant impact on the world investment. China began introducing foreign investment since reform and opening-up and the actual utilized FDI amounted to US $2.26 billion only in 1983. While after 1992, China became the developing country with the largest foreign investment inflow. Since 2002, China has been listed in the top three countries in utilizing FDI in the world, and ranks the 6th in 2007 in the world in attracting FDI. From 2001-2008, the actual utilized FDI in China was US $504.3 billion and annually US $ 63 billion. In 2008, this figure was US $95.25 billion, 41 times of that in 1983; and the FDI hit US $ 92.4 billion up by 99.4 times. The number of foreign funded firms increased from 7 in 1980 to 280,000 in the end of 2007. The industry structure of foreign investment is also multiple, covering varied fields from the common manufacturing to basic industries, infrastructure construction as well as the high-tech industries like the R&D center, integrated circuit, computer and communication products etc.

China's overseas direct investments have been gradually expanded since 2000, indicating a significant improvement on China's ability to participate in the international economic cooperation. China's non-financial overseas direct investment was only US $2.9 billion in 2003, and increased by more than 10 times by 2008 to US $40.7 billion. Now, more than 7,000 domestic investors have established over 10,000 firms in over 170 countries and regions throughout the world by overseas direct investing, with the invested fields being greatly broadened and the level upgraded. Resources, telecommunications, petrochemicals, financial etc. have been the major fields in China's overseas investments. Many overseas R&D centers and industrial agglomerations have been built, and the establishing of overseas economic and trade cooperative zones has been promoted substantially. By the end of 2008, China has become the world's biggest foreign exchange reserve holder by an amount of US $1.9 trillion, providing a strong basis for overseas investments. Overseas investments help strengthen the international competitiveness of Chinese firms and 35 Chinese firms were listed as the *World Fortune 500 Companies* in 2008.

1.3. China: A Developing Market Economy

From 1978 to 2009, China has witnessed a rapid marketization process and a historic transition from a planned economy to a market economy. With reference of the Heritage Foundation's economic liberalization index, we have launched a whole set of index system, which describes the primary aspects of a market economy and evaluate the marketization degree of China's economy using annual data. Our calculation results of the degree of China' market development are: 2.51 or 69%[10] by 2000 and 77.7%[11] by 2006. It means that China's marketization has reached around 70% with 100% being assumed as a complete market economy criteria and indicates that a market economy framework has been established in China. Actually we herein take 60% as the preset threshold value of being a market economy. According to this criteria, any country with a marketization degree higher than 60% can be called a market economy. An economy with a marketization degree between 60%-80% is defined as a mature market economy. China's index value in 2006 is much higher than 60%, which means China is already a market economy and meanwhile stepping into the stage of a mature market economy. Correspondingly, 77 countries have acknowledged China's full market economy status by the year 2008.

China is a developing market economy, which has two aspects of implications. First, China is during the course of transition from a primary market economy into a mature market economy, which stresses the degree of maketization under the same system. Thirty years ago, China was unable to develop its market economy because it did not choose to develop a market economy in the first place. Market economy, as an economic pattern with the most liberalized growth, can be developed rapidly once chosen as a country's economic pattern, especially in today's economic globalization.

Second, it is as a developing country that China is adopting a market economy system. This is in line with the meaning of 'development' in the subject of 'Economics of Development'. The concept of a developing market economy is better understood from the economic development point of view. Indeed, the difference between 'development' and 'advanced' not only refers to the disparity of economic development between the developing countries and developed countries, but also implies different social systems adopted. In this sense, China need to work hard to catch up with the developed countries and sustain rapid, stable and healthy economic development, in order to lay a solid foundation for the market economy.

---

[10] Institute of Economic and Resources Management of Beijing Normal University. *A Report On the Development of China's Market Economy 2003*. China International Commerce and Trade Press, 2003, P217.

[11] Institute of Economic and Resources Management of Beijing Normal University. A Report On the Development of China's Market Economy 2008. Beijing Normal University Publishing House, 2008, P204.

Now, it becomes obvious that the judgment of developing market economy is made from the perspectives of both economic development and social system combined. In this view, the development and reform supplement each other. Only if the economy is developed into a certain stage, the market economy system can be established and perfected. Meanwhile the full establishment of the market economy provides an important system preparation for a rapid economic growth.

In April, 1998, EU deleted China from the list of non-market economies under its anti-dumping policies, giving China the treatment as a special market economy between the 'non-market economies' and 'market economies', which indicates EU timely adjusted its judgment about China's market economy status. Peter Mandelson, the UK Business Secretary and former EU Trade Commissioner, said that talks over granting China the "market economy status" should not be held back politically out of the prejudice or special trade interests in Europe[12]. On July 28th , 2009, Chinese Vice Premier Wang Qishan stated at the *China-US Strategic and Economic Dialogue* that China and US should work together now on overcoming difficulties caused by the financial crisis and urged US to recognize China's market economy status as early as possible[13].

---

[12] Source: Xinhua News Agency, Shenzhen Branch, Sep.10, 2009.

[13] Source: Xinhua News Agency, Washington, July 28, 2009.

Chapter 2

EXPERIENCE: RISING FROM THE PLANNED ECONOMY

People are wondering how China became an emerging market. Certainly, the importance of its reform and opening-up therein over the past 30 years can never be overemphasized because it is the key for China to have stepped from a planned economy into an emerging market. In this part , such topics will be discussed as China's main reform phases, China's experience in reform and development and China's difficulties in its economic and social development.

2.1. FIVE PHASES OF CHINA'S REFORM

As an emerging market economy, China has been reforming its economic system for 30 years and been through several stages of reform and development. The shift it made from an planned economy to an emerging market economy involves several phases.

Phase One

During the early reform and opening-up from 1978 to 1985, breakthroughs were made in the rural areas, the state-owned-firms carried out decentralization and interest concession, the urban and rural commodity markets revived and Special Economic Zones were established in the coastal areas.

China's economic system reform made breakthrough in rural areas first. In 1978, "*Baochandaohu*" (Fixing of farm output quotas for each household) began to emerge quietly in some rural places in China, which broke the necessity of collective production under the planned economy for a long time. *Baochandaohu* was promoted as early as in the 1960s, but was put to an end after considered by Chairman Mao as a capitalist practice. This time, Deng Xiaoping was resolutely in favor of it. Up to the end of 1983, *Baochandaohu* that is mainly in the form of household accounts for 90% of China's peasant households. It is believed to be a breakthrough in China's reform and has also greatly furthered the development of the rural economy. From 1978-1984, China's gross agricultural output increased by 55.4% and the grain output by 33.6%. From 1978-1983, rural expenditure per capita had increased by RMB 108[1] and the living standard of rural residents being greatly improved. In the beginning of 1979, the rural fair trade was resumed and the farmers allowed to trade their agricultural products, and hence, the farmers were greatly motivated and the rural markets thrived.

State-Owned Enterprises in China began to reform, too. Under the planned economy, the government was in charge of the firms' production, distribution, property and employee. Now, many of these things are left to the firms themselves by power decentralization and interest concessions. For example, firms were allowed to retain some profit after tax payment for better development. Enlarging the decision-making power of firms improved the initiatives of firms, their return and the national fiscal income eventually.

The opening-up started with the establishment of Special Economic Zones (SEZs). From 1978 to 1983, 4 SEZs were established in China, indicating the first crucial step of the opening-up. The firms in SEZs were exempted customs and enjoyed the lower income tax rates. Foreign high technology products were allowed to sell in mainland. The scope and coverage of the adjustments by markets were much broader. Many management skills were learned from Hong Kong. With the development of the export-oriented economy, the outward economic activities were burgeoning. These SEZs served as the 'pacemaker', 'laboratory' and 'window' for the subsequent national reform and opening-up.

---

[1] Source: Calculated with the reference of the data of *China Statistical Yearbook 2008*.

Phase Two

Phase 2 began from October 1984 and until the end of 1991. There are some major achievements.

The deepening of rural reform: town and village enterprises (TVEs) emerged as a new force and grain purchase-and-sale system reform began. In this period, the development of the town and village enterprises (TVEs) was the focus. In 1984, the firms run by rural communes were renamed as TVEs. In those 7 years, the gross output and profit of TVEs rose by a dozen and even several dozen times, while with a naturally fluctuating growth rate. The controlled grain purchasing and marketing system existing for a long time in the planned economy was also reformed. In 1985, the state monopoly purchase system of grain was replaced by market order system which was intended to purchase grain based on the market price instead of the fixed price by cost. In the mean time, the ban on the sale of extra grain was relaxed and farmers were given some decision-making power for marketing.

Opening wider to the outside world: 14 coastal cities were opened and Hainan was established to a separate province. In 1984, after inspecting the SEZs, Deng Xiaoping suggested further opening the coastal cities. In May 1984, 14 coastal cities including Tianjin, Shanghai, Guangzhou etc. were opened officially, with their autonomous economic power expanded and preferential policies provided for foreign investors, which represents the further expansion and spread of China's overall opening-up. At the First Session of the 7th NPC in 1988, sanction was given to the establishment of Hainan Province and Hainan Island was designated as the Hainan Special Economic Zone, the biggest SEZ of China.

Phase Three

The period 1992-2001 saw the initial establishment of the socialist market economy in China. In 1992, the Communist Party of China explicitly set the socialist market economy system as a goal for the economic system reform. From then on, the market reform has been carried out forcefully. The main reform includes:

The Deepening of SOEs' reform. After 1992, the transformation into the joint-stock system became the major form of SOE's reform. In the mean time, with the focus of the reform shifting from invigorating one single SOE to invigorating the overall state-owned economy, a lot of large and highly competitive firms and groups emerged, and their transformation in business operation system was promoted as well as the profits increased.

The position of private economy rose from 'complementary' to 'important component'. At the 15th National Congress of the CPC in 1997, it was pointed out that "private economy is an important component of the socialist market economy", which represented a new historic breakthrough in the theory of ownership system. An amendment to the Constitution, ratified in 1999, clarified the position and role of the non-state economy, such as individual and private economy etc.

The government' role in management has been altered greatly, and China's macro-economic control system has taken shape initially. In the beginning of 1994, a major reform aimed at the establishment of macro-economy control system started. The contents of the fiscal and tax reform in 1994 were to sort out the relationship between the central and local governments, reform the profit distribution system of SOEs and reform the tax system, which improved the simple decentralization and interest concessions through defining the fiscal power by the public role of the governments at all levels. At the national conference on finance work 1998, it was requested to establish a public finance system. In 1994, the State Development Bank of China (SDBC), the Export-Import Bank of China and China Agricultural Development Bank were established successively, separating the policy banks from commercial ones. The Law of the People's Bank of China effective in 1995 established that the People's Bank of China was the central bank.

Phase Four

Phase 4 was from the end of 2001 through 2007. At the end of 2001, China officially became the 143rd member country of WTO, which represents a new era of China's opening-up. Through thoroughly implementing its commitments, China has deepened its market reform continuously with growing marketization in all fields. The marketization is improved in the following aspects.

Further marketization of the production factors. As for the marketization of labor force, the Chinese government has long stood back from the allocation of the labor resource, leaving it more and more to the market itself instead of the public administration. As for the capitalization, QFII (qualified foreign institutional investor), share structure reform and QDII (Qualified domestic institutional investor) were implemented successively after 2002, which indicates constant improvements of the stock market. At the same time, equity market, mediate and small firms sector, Stock Transfer Agent System were established successively and has been making impressive progress. As for the land marketization, there were a series of regulations introduced: *Provisions on the assignment of the right to the use of state-owned land by means of bidding, auction, and listing* and *Provisions on agreed assignment of the right to the use of state-owned land* by the Ministry of Land and Resources (2002), *Decision on deepening reform and strict land management* by the State Council (2004). Hence, a market mechanism was initiated for the price of land-use right.

Share the fruit of marketization reform, reform the income distribution system and improve the social security system gradually. At the 17th National Congress of the CPC in 2007, it was stated that equitable income distribution is an important indicator for the social equity. We should adhere to and improve the distribution system which encompasses the distribution by work mainly. We should ensure the factors of production such as labor, capital, technology and managerial expertise to be distributed according to their respective contribution. The relation between the efficiency and equity in both primary distribution and redistribution should be handled properly, with particular emphasis given to the equity in redistribution. We should gradually increase the share of personal income in the distribution of national income, and raise the share of work remuneration in the primary distribution. Vigorous efforts should be made to raise the income of low-income groups, to increase poverty-reduction aid and the minimum wage, and to set up a mechanism of regular pay increases for employees and salary payments. Conditions should be promoted to enable more people having property income. We should protect lawful incomes, regulate excessively high incomes and ban illegal gains. We should increase transfer payments, intensify the income regulation through taxation, break business monopolies, create equal opportunities, rectify the distribution order and stop the income disparity from growing.

Phase Five

The global financial crisis began in 2008 has affected China's economic development as well as its economic reform. Can we deny the capitalism just because the crisis started in the United States and Europe? Is China's transition to the market-oriented economy wrong? It is an ongoing debate around the world especially in China, which in the meantime may indicate another phase for China's reform.

We hold that stressing the role of governments and of the state-owned economy against the crisis can be only a temporary approach and by which the market economy system will only be perfected rather than denied. Only by the reform and opening-up can China secure its position in globalization, promote the harmonious development of the economy and society and achieve sustained development eventually. The 17th National Congress of the CPC addressed the marketization from the perspective of industrialization, urbanization, marketization, informatization and internationalization combined, which demonstrates the government's resolution and confidence in the economic reform.

2.2. Experiences of Economic Reform and Development

China's reform and opening-up has shifted it from a planned economy to a market economy, with the economy being developed and lots of experiences earned. The successful experiences include the following five aspects.

Firstly, Leading Reform Requires the Courage to Abandon Traditional Ideology

To make China shift from a planned economy to a market economy, the top national leaders' determination on the reform is crucial. For instance, China would not make any real step forward in the reform if the leaders ignored the reality, misjudged the role of capital, regarded the capitalists as exploiters, banned the cooperation between different social classes and persisted in annihilating the private economy.

Secondly, A Country's Management System and Institutions Should Be Suitable for and Helpful to the Development of Productivity

Decades of practical experiences show that if a country's management system is not suitable for its productivity condition, its economy will suffer stagnation or even retrogress, and vice versa. The rule of economic development also suggests that the government is playing a vital role in promoting economic development. The combined efforts from the government and its people, the coordination of macroeconomic controls and microeconomic activities as well as the cooperation of national capital and private capital can guarantee a country's economic development. It is exceedingly important how the government sees its roles and improves its leadership and efficiency continuously.

Thirdly, Good Economic Relations with Foreign Countries Is Vital for Domestic Economic Development

International political and economic environment is essential for a country's economic development. Developing the economy in a closed environment is prone to being conservative and complacent, and blocking the way of progress. By contrast, developing the economy in an open environment, facing pressures from outside markets and seeing great accomplishments of other countries will help a country find its own weakness and get motivated for progresses. China opened up to the outside world after 1978 and introduced foreign capital, advanced technology and management skills. With the import and export volume rapidly expanding, China has increased its economic communications and exchanges with the outside world, which has accelerated its economic growth greatly.

Fourthly, Economic Reform and Legislation Construction Complement Each Other

China has been facing many legal problems during the reform and opening-up and the resolution requires the combinative perspectives of both economics and law. On one hand, we need to set up rules for the market economy in order to protect and preserve the results of economic reforms. On the other hand, regulations are needed to restrict and improve the administrative power in turn. China has already established an intact market economic and legal system, including the legal system for market entities, those regulating the activities of market entities and controlling the macroeconomy. Nevertheless, China's legal system for the market economy is still far from perfection.

Finally, Adhering to the Principle of Sustainable Growth Is Vital

Evaluating the result of the economic development requires looking into the economic output factors not only such as the economic growth, but also the input factors. Less input and more output is good , but it is more important to sustain the input and output. The Chinese government has made tremendous efforts to protect the environment and save energies for years, but there is still a long way to go to reach the sustainable growth goals. History shows that people not only need money, but also fresh air, clean water and good living conditions for their offspring, which is now the priority for every country. China has a long way to go to develop a green economy and to fulfill a coordinated development at all levels.

2.3. Challenges China Face for Further Economic and Social Development

There are big issues currently existing in China and could not be solved in 5-10 years. Here might be several examples:

Issues on Income Disparity

The distribution of national income is always the first and foremost issue of the economy. Now the income disparity, with the growth of Chinese economy, is getting more and more evident.

First, from the perspective of aggregate income distribution in China, the data of National Bureau of Statistics (NBS) [2] show that China's Gini Coefficient jumps from 0.317 in 1987 to 0.438 in 2007. As for the urban-rural income gap, from 1997-2007, the income of the highest-income group (RMB 9,304) is 1.64 times of that of the lowest-income group (RMB 5,667) in urban area; whereas the income of the highest-income group (RMB 3,972) is 2.41 times of the lowest-income group (RMB 1,648) in rural area. The nominal urban-rural income gap ratio increases from 2.57:1 (1978) to 3.32:1 (2007). Furthermore, the income gap among regions is widening. In 2007, per capita GDP of Western China is merely 41.47% of that of Eastern China. The income disparity among sectors is huge, too: in 2007, average income of the highest-income sector, securities industry, is 14.49 times of that of the lowest-income sector, agriculture.

The main reasons for a widening income disparity lie in that: (1) With the market mechanism adjusting the primary distribution of national income, the factor income disparity is widening, and so is that among the regions. (2) Effects of redistribution by fiscal policy barely show up. (3) The Illegal and off-the-book income is out of control. The distribution beyond system deteriorates the income disparity.

Although the government is making significant adjustments on the income distribution, and a social security system is under way, the income disparity is difficult to eliminate in the future 5-10 years.

Issue of Modernization of Chinese Farmers

The introduction of urbanization, urban and rural integrated planning and construction of new village are all intended to improve the life quality and to modernize the production pattern of the farmers.

It's key to increase the income of rural residents. Data show that the development of 800 million farmers is the bottleneck for China to reach the income level of mid-ranking developed countries (per capita GDP US $8,000) in the middle of the century. In 2007, the average income of 600 million urban residents is US $1,767.32, whereas that of 700 million rural residents is only US $530.82.[3] The 16th National Congress states the goal that the GDP of 2020

[2] Source: Calculated with the data from *China Statistical Yearbook* and *China Rural Statistical Yearbook* over the years.

[3] Source: Calculated with the data from *China Statistical Yearbook 2008.*

quadruples that of 2000 and hence brings forward the goal that per capita GDP of 2020 quadruples that of 2000, which means an average growth rate of 5.4% per annum.

To increase the income of farmers, it's important to arrange rural workers to work in town. However, with urban-rural labor market being segmented at present, rural workers can hardly enjoy the equal citizen treatment. Due to numerous reasons, only 30% of rural workers signs employment contract. In contrast, over 95% urban workers sign employment contracts with State-owned Enterprises (SOEs), Collective Firms, and Foreign Investment Firms. During January to September of 2008, the ratio of workers with contracts signed reaches 93% in the industrial enterprises above designated size, which was below 20% before the implementation of *the Labor Contract Law*. Some local governments merely change the rural *hukou* (the identity control policy of the Chinese government) of farmers to urban *hukou* and confiscate the lands from farmers for higher urbanization without regard to the employment and social security of these farmers. There are numerous issues to be tackled step by step.

Reform on Administrative System of Government

The key to reform on administrative system of Chinese government is how to deal with the relationship between government and market. First, government needs position itself. A good positioning prevents the cross boundary activities. Otherwise, the market adjustment activities will be left to administrative intervention, which used to appear frequently in the process of reform and development. The administrative system of government is affected by three types of government positioning: The first is the relationship between big and small governments, which is about the administrative scope and the function of governments. The second is the one between strong and weak governments. It means the administrative intensity and how governments should do. The third is the one between good and bad governments, which involves how the public evaluate the administrative capability and performance.

Three important relationships need to be tackled: first, upper-down relationship, namely the relationship between the central and local government; second, left-right relationship, namely coordination among different departments; third, the upper-down and left-right relationship at all vertical and horizontal levels. From top down, there are relationships between different levels of the government and residents; from left to right, there are relationships among provinces, among cities and among firms etc.

These issues have not yet been solved so far during the reform, because the government is just getting to recognize its functional position. Between the choice of government or market, the government usually tended to the administrative methods for faster effect, hence many issues have accumulated.

Sustainable Issue of Economic Growth

The developing countries have made significant progress on poverty reduction and economic development but with heavy costs: air pollution is worsening, fresh water is increasingly scarce, soil desertification is accelerating, forest destruction is out of control, biodiversity is fading away and fishery is shrinking etc.. Therefore, it's necessary to tackle economic development and environment issues altogether in order to solve the sustainable development problem.

The topic of *World Development Report 2010*[4] is development and climate change, and it recommends building a *climate-smart world*. The developing countries can shift to low-carbon growth pattern to pursue development and reduce poverty, which demands financial and technical support from the developed countries; the developed countries should reduce carbon emission immediately, and it calls for cooperation among all countries to promote global sustainable development.

Chinese government is also emphasizing a sustainable development, the environmental protection and resource saving, but in reality, the tendency to pursue GDP growth solely is hard to stop. The key lies in the lack of the expression of public opinion on specific issues and the local governments would rather sacrifice the environment for growth. It's a vital issue, while impossible to be solved in a short term.

Coordination and Interaction between Domestic and Foreign Economy

International relationship is sophisticated, with both advantages and disadvantages. From making two-way exchange of the capital and technology

---

4 Source: from *World Development Report 2010*, the World Bank, September of 2009.

to considering the opinions from international society and coordinating the domestic policies with those of the big international players, China has made a big step forward.

Post-international financial crisis is placing the global economy at a new equilibrium. International relationship, de facto, the coordination of national interests with each other, is getting more difficult, while more important. The differences of strength and attitude between the developed and developing countries is just one of the difficulties. Currently, the number of projects in need of international coordination is increasing, instead of reducing; particularly the issue of global environment which is getting more and more complicated, takes more time for coordination. It needs a long term from bringing forward a problem, coordinating relationship to negotiation and communication.

Chapter 3

PERFORMANCE: TACKLING THE GLOBAL FINANCIAL CRISIS

As an emerging market, China is different from the developed countries in handling the global financial crisis in following three aspects: first, it is less affected because the financial derivatives and leverage are relatively slow in an emerging market; second, its overall economy sustains a positive growth; third, its measures work faster. Nevertheless, while there are still uncertainties about the world economy, China should keep alert against possible new difficulties in its economy. Next, we will look at the impact of the global financial crisis on China, China's countermeasures and effects, and so on.

3.1. IMPACTS OF THE GLOBAL FINANCIAL CRISIS ON CHINA

Since the 3rd quarter of 2008, China has been subject to growing influence of the global financial crisis.

First, the economy slowed down. The *China MonthlyEconomic Indicators* showed that the cumulative quarterly GDP growth rate in 2008 dropped sharply, with 10.6%, 10.4%, 9.9%, and 9% for Q1, Q1-Q2, Q1-Q3 and Q1-Q4 respectively.

If we take a long-term view, China's economy had a hard time in 2008 undoubtedly (see Figure 1).

As shown in Figure 1, in the past 5 years, an inflection point appeared in 2007 in China's economy. China's GDP had two-digit growth from 2004 to

2007, with 10.1%, 10.4%, 11.6%, 13.0% respectively. However, it fell to one-digit growth of 9% in 2008.

Secondly, the export volume plunged. In the fourth quarter of 2008, the orders of the export firms in Southeastern China decreased sharply and even got suspended, and some firms suffered business stagnation, which exhibited an unexpectedly rapid downslide. As the financial crisis spreads, the import and export volume of China dropped sharply (see Figure 2).

As shown in Figure 2, both the commodity export and import in 2008 increased slightly year on year but with a sharp drop in the growth rate. From 2004 to 2007, the growth of China's export and import were 35.7%, 23.2%, 23.8% and 23.5% respectively, yet for 2008, it was only 17.8%, down by 5.7%.

Thirdly, the unemployment rate rose sharply. Factories went bankrupt and more workers lost jobs as the export decreased. In late 2008, China's urban and town unemployment registered 4.2%, up by 0.2% than 2007, while continuous improvement had been made on the unemployment before. By the end of 2008, 20 million of 130 million rural workers have lost jobs and gone home.[1]

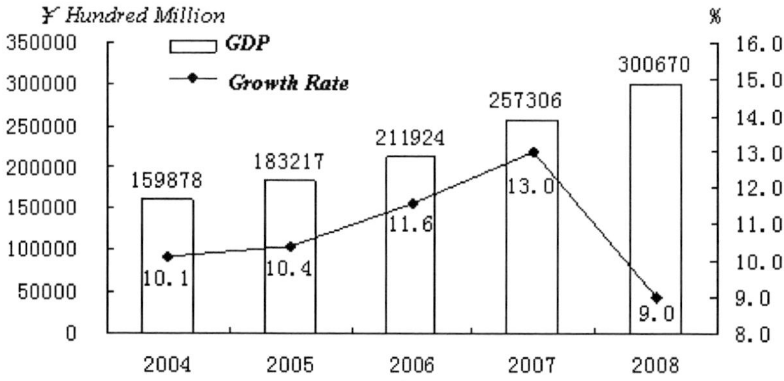

Source: Statistical Communiqué of the People's Republic of China on the 2008 National Economic and Social Development.

Figure 1. Chinese GDP Volume and Growth 2004 -2008.

[1] Chen Jiagui. *China's Economic Prospect: Report of Spring, 2009*: P4. Beijing: Social Science Literature Press, April, 2009.

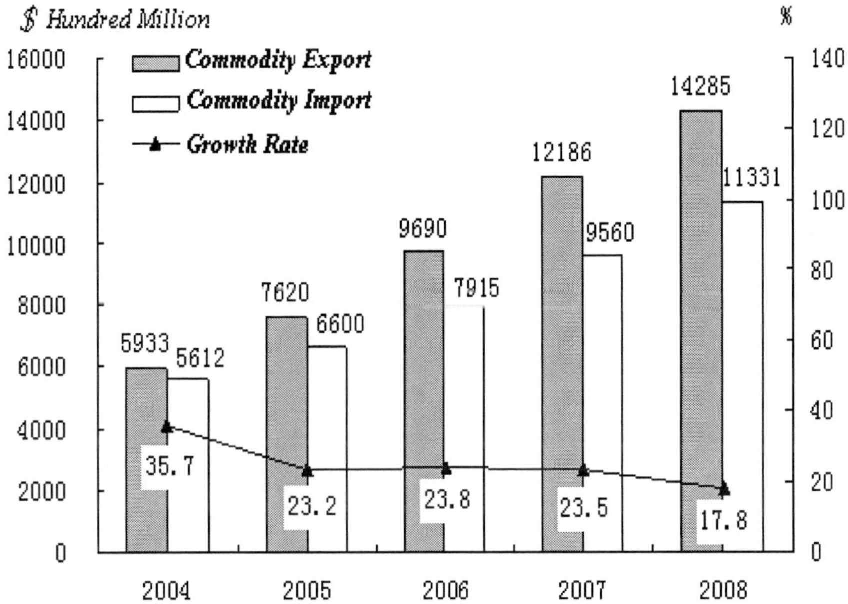

Source: Statistical Communiqué of the People's Republic of China on the 2008 National Economic and Social Development.

Figure 2. China's Commodity Export and Import Volume and Growth.

3.2. Macroeconomic Policies and Measures to Prevent the Economy from Getting Worse

Chinese government took active actions to tackle the global financial crisis and introduced a series of countermeasures to sustain the growth, enlarge domestic demand and adjust the economic structure. Proactive fiscal and moderately easy monetary policies were introduced to prevent the economic downslide and secure the growth; ten measures such as the home appliance subsidy program for rural areas and those in favor of rural finance were introduced to enlarge domestic demand; *Ten Major Industry Revival Plans* were presented to encourage innovation and technology R&D, save energy and turn the economic structure to be more green.

In the First Place, China Carried out Proactive Fiscal Policies and Moderately Easy Monetary Policies

Proactive fiscal policies include four aspects. Firstly, the investment by the central government will guide the local fund. Of the RMB 4 trillion stimulus plan, the central government will invest RMB 1.18 trillion, with the rest to be made by local governments. Secondly, advance the reform on tax and charge to cut tax structurally. Implement the VAT by consumption to ease the tax burden of the firms. Reform the tax and charge of the product oil to promote energy saving and emission reduction. Thirdly, optimize the fiscal expenditure structure with a predominance given to social security system and improvement on the basic living conditions. Fourthly, technology innovation, energy saving and emission-reduction will be supported help facilitate the economic structure adjustment and economic growth transformation.

Moderately easy monetary policies contain five aspects[2]. First, ensure the financial system liquidity and provide financial institutions with liquidity support in time. Second, keep an appropriately increasing credit, strengthen the role of the bank credit in the economic development, relax the restrictions to the credit scale by commercial banks and enlarge the credit scale appropriately. Third, strengthen discount-window guidance and policy steering and optimize the loan structure. Fourth, further develop the financing function of the security market. Fifth, improve the financial services of the central bank.

Furthermore, Complementary Measures for Enlarging the Domestic Demand Were Enforced

Chinese government introduced ten major measures[3] to further expand the domestic demand and stimulate the economy. First, accelerate basic housing projects. Second, speed up infrastructure construction in rural areas. Third, speed up major infrastructure construction projects such as railways, highways

[2] Source: Website of PBC, *Implement the moderately easy monetary policy and further enlarge domestic demand to promote the economic growth,* http://www.pbc.gov.cn/detail.asp?col=100&ID=2914.

[3] Source: *Measures for enlarging domestic demand and promoting economic growth arranged on State Council executive meeting,* http://www.gov.cn/ldhd/2008-11/09/ content_1143689.htm.

and airports, etc. Fourth, accelerate the development of health care, culture and education. Fifth, strengthen the environment protection. Sixth, encourage independent innovation and structural adjustment. Seventh, step up the post-earthquake reconstruction of the affected areas. Eighth, raise the income of both urban and rural households. Ninth, implement the reform on value added tax in all areas and industries, encourage enterprises to make technological transformation, and ease the burden of the firms by RMB 120 billion. Tenth, reinforce the financial support to the economic development. By the end of 2010, an investment of RMB 4 trillion will be required to complete the above projects.

Moreover, many ministries and commissions also introduced some relevant measures. China's Banking Regulatory Commision has relaxed the bank entry to rural areas, in order to promote rural finance, offer better services for rural construction and explore potential consumption of rural households. By the end of June 2009, 118 rural financial institutions have been opened, taking in RMB 4.733 billion capital and RMB 13.1 billion of deposit. Those institutions have issued RMB 5.5 billion loans for farmers and RMB 8.2 billion for small and medium firms. [4] *Overall Work Plan for New-type Rural Financial Institutions 2009-2011* by China's Banking Regulatory Commission has been approved by the State Council, under which 1,300 rural financial institutions of new-type will be set up in the coming 3 years. China's Ministry of Commerce carried out *Home Appliance Subsidy Program for Rural Areas* to stimulate the rural consumption and domestic demand.

Finally, Make Adjustment to Economic Structure through Industrial Policies

The *Ten Major Industry Revival Plans* are intended to encourage the products that are energy-saving, environment-friendly, clean and with high added value. The ten plans are as follows. (1) Auto industry revival plan. Restructure auto industry, encourage independent innovation and technology improvement and implement the new energy auto strategy. (2) Iron and steel industry revival plan. Control the aggregate output, encourage corporation reorganization and strengthen the technological improvement with supports to R&D and technology introduction. (3) Textile industry revival plan. Focus on

[4] Source: the website of China's Banking Regulatory Commission, http://www.cbrc.gov.cn/chinese/home/jsp/index.jsp

independent innovation, phase out backward technology, optimize layout and then push forward the industry adjustment and upgrade. (4) Equipment manufacturing industry revival plan. Strengthen independent innovation by investing more on technology improvement. (5) Ship manufacturing industry revival plan. Control the increasing of manufacturing capacity and promote the structure adjustment. (6) Petroleum chemical industry plan. Adjust industry structure, optimize industrial layout, enhance innovation ability and management skill to acquire more competitiveness. (7) Light industry revival plan. Further implement the *Home Appliance Subsidy Program for Rural Areas* and expand the subsidy. (8) Nonferrous metal industry revival plan. Strictly control the output and phase out the backward production capacity. (9) Electronic and information industry revival plan. Enhance independent innovation and perfect the development environment. (10) Logistics industry revival plan. Accelerate corporation reorganization and build up large logistics firms which can offer quality services and compete globally.

Meanwhile, some commercial banks such as the Industrial and Commercial Bank of China (ICBC) and China Merchants Bank(CMB) etc. issued *green loans*. Through strictly checking the borrowers' capability on clean and energy-saving technology and the extent of the production pollution problems, priority will be given to those environment-friendly and clean energy projects. Many firms have started seeking green production plans. Take Geely Auto. Geely sticks to an environment-friendly standard as the prerequisite of the whole production process, from material selection, assembling to emission design.

3.3. Effects of China's Economic Stimulus Policies[5]

The Chinese government adopted a package of effective policies and measures, which has helped sustain a stable economic growth.

[5] Unless otherwise stated, data in this section are from the official website of National Bureau of Statistics of China.

The Economy Is Stabilizing and GDP Growth Rate Is Back Again to the Upward Trend

The data show that China's economy is stabilizing: in the first half of 2009, the total fixed asset investment grew by 33.5% in volume and by 7.2% in growth rate year-on-year ; GDP grew by 7.1%, up by 1% than during the first quarter of 2009. The second quarter alone saw a GDP growth rate of 7.9%, up by 1.8% than the first quarter.

The Employment Is Generally Stable

During the first half of 2009, 5.69 million new jobs were created in the urban area, completing 63% of the full-year target; at the end of the 2nd quarter of 2009, the number of rural workers increased by 3.78 million, 2.6% higher year on year.

Consumers' Confidence Has Gradually Increased

The domestic-demand-expanding policy has been remarkably effective in improving the urban and rural household income and expanding the domestic demand through increasing the investment on the projects related to people's lives. According to a survey by National Bureau of Statistics of China, the per capita disposable income of urban households was RMB 8,856 in the first half of 2009, up by a real growth of 11.2% YOY which was 4.9 % higher than last year. The total retail sales of consumer goods nominally increased by 15.0%, down by 6.4% than last year, and the real growth rate was16.6%, 3.7% higher than the same period of last year.

The Efforts on Energy Conservation Have Begun to Take Effects

In recent years, China's energy consumption of unit GDP(RMB per ten thousand) was going down year by year: the year 2006, 2007 and 2008 saw a decrease of 1.79%, 4.04% and 4.59% respectively, the first quarter of 2009 saw a 2.89% decrease compared with the same period of last year[6].

3.4. A Comprehensive Assessment on the Current Difficulties

Since there are still uncertainties about the recovery of China's economy and the economic basis is not yet stable, we need to assess the current difficulties: the bubbles in the real estate and stock markets cannot be ignored; the increase in rural households' income is slow and the rural demand is still weak; the decline in the export and the problem of overcapacity are already evident.

The Bubbles in the Real Estate Market and Stock Market Can Not Be Ignored

In July 2009, China Banking Regulatory Commission ordered the banks to ensure that the new loans flow to the real economy rather than the stock or real estate market, to strictly monitor the destination of the loans and strengthen loan risk control. However, in the first half of 2009, the bank loans rose by RMB 7.37 trillion[7], three times as much as that of last year, and even higher by 47% than the full-year target made by the central government From the beginning of this year to the end of July, Shanghai Stock Exchange Composite Index has risen by more than 88%, making China the fastest growing major stock market this year. Meanwhile, in the real estate market, the real estate investment rose by 9.9% YOY in the first half of this year, the housing sales grew by 31.7%, and the National Real Estate Development Climate Index in June was 96.55. Without a corresponding increase in the household income, the significant growth in the housing sales and the soaring prices against the sluggish business inevitably indicates the bubbles.

---

6 Source: National Economic and Social Development Statistical Communiquй of every calendar year.

7 Source: Website of PBC, *The credit amount grew rapidly and the liquidity of bank system kept sufficient,* http://www.pbc.gov.cn/detail.asp?col=100&ID=3299

The Rural Household Income Increases Slowly, Resulting to the Weak Rural Demand

Both the total income of the farmers and their wage income grow slowly or at a declining rate. In the first half of 2009, the per capita cash income of rural households was the lowest growth level in the past 5 years. The price plunge of the agricultural produce and the difficulties for farmers to work outside leads to the slow income growth. The sharp fall in the income growth of rural households and a widening income disparity between urban and rural households will certainly weaken the rural demand with insufficient leverage, thereby hindering further recovery of the national economy.

The Decline in Export and the Problem of Overcapacity Is Evident

The global economic downturn drew down the major orders and affected China's exports and employment in turn. From November 2008 to June 2009, China's export maintained a negative growth for eight consecutive months. According to the figures released by China's General Administration of Customs, in the first half of this year, China's aggregate import and export value amounts to US $946.12 billion, down by 23.5%. The accumulated trade surplus was US $96.94 billion, down by 1.3% or US $1.3 billion net. With the new type of trade protectionism coming back worldwide, China's foreign trade is still facing many difficulties. At the same time, in the first half of 2009, China's Consumer Price Index (CPI) fell by 1.1%, in which it fell by 1.7% in June; Producer's Price Index for Manufactured Products (PPI) fell by 5.9%, in which it fell by 7.8% in June.[8] The declining price reflects insufficient effective demand and the relative surplus of supply. It is estimated that the problem of overcapacity will get worse in the second half of the year.

---

[8] Source: *State Council Information Office of P.R. China held press conference on national economic situation of the 1st half of 2009*, http://www.scio.gov.cn/xwfbh/xwbfbh/wqfbh/2009/0716a/.

Chapter 4

TREND: NEW ROLES IN INTERNATIONAL ECONOMY

Looking forward, as a fast-growing emerging market, China will definitely contribute more to and play new roles in the international economy as a new world-class market, an ideal investment destination, a new global investor, and a builder of the new international financial order.

4.1. A NEW WORLD-CLASS MARKET

China is known as a factory of the world, while we will see that China is turning to a large world-class market, based on five principal elements: (1) A large domestic market. As a big country with 1.3 billion people, China has a lower-than-median GDP per capita among the middle-income nations and limited purchasing power per person. Nonetheless, any small number, when multiplied by 1.3 billion, will become extremely large. (2) The domestic demand is multivariate. The Chinese household income structure is complicated and there is huge disparity in ladder-shaped distribution, leading to a multivariate domestic demand. (3) The urban consumer group is expanding gradually. (4) There is huge space for promoting rural consumption level. 800 million farmers in China only consume a third of the national commodities and the expenditure is only a quarter of the urban level, indicating great potentials for further improvement. (5) Various emerging consumption patterns are burgeoning out. G*reen consumption* is sought after; *credit consumption* is becoming a fashion; *on-line consumption* is growing in popularity and *leasing consumption* will expand greatly. All these show that the Chinese market has palpable advantages with fairly strong market absorption. Nearly every commodity category from any country all over the world could find a certain market share in China.

The world will be exhilarated when China could import as much as US $1trillion. The day is in the near future. The robust growth of the China economy is promoting the personal income level and enlarging the potential of national consumption rate. Next, we will analyze the consumption potential of Chinese households.

Since the reform and opening-up 30 years ago, GDP per capita of China has been on the rise and the household income and wealth been growing rapidly (See Figure 3).

As Figure 3 shows, China's GDP per capita has increased from RMB 381 in 1978 to RMB 22,640 in 2008, up by 60 times than 30 years ago. On the other hand, however, the saving rate of Chinese households has declined from 62.1% in 1978 to 42.8% in 2008. China is now adjusting the economic structure. To expand the domestic demand, China needs to promote the household income level and consumption rate where huge potential lies.

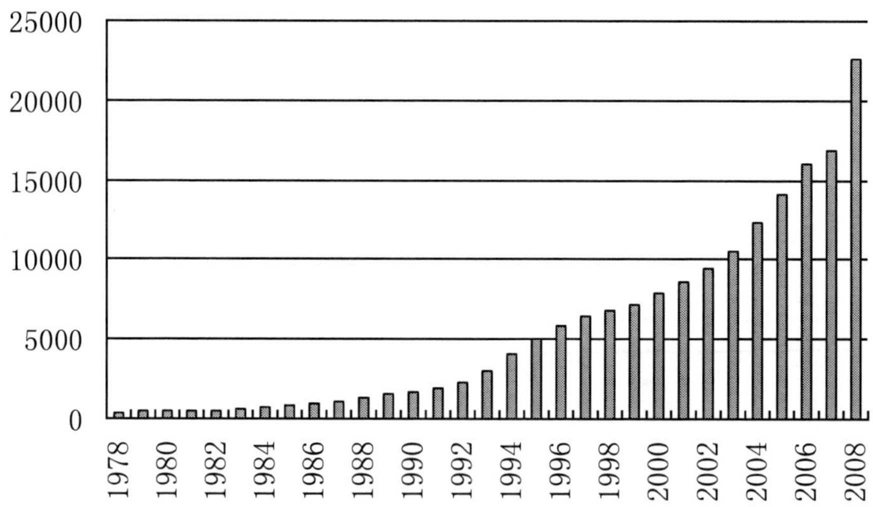

Source: Data of 2008 extracted from "*Chinese National Economy and Social Development Statistic Report 2008*"; other data from "*Chinese Statistic Book 2008*".

Figure 3. Per capita GDP in China, 1978-2008 (Unit: RMB).

Table 2. Comparison on Indicators of China 2007-2008 with the U.S Related Data (Unit: %)

	China	China	United States	United States
Indicators	Year	Data	Data	Year
Ratio of Secondary Industry in GDP	2008	48.8	38	1950-1960
Ratio of Employment in the Secondary Industry	2007	26.8	30	1900
Ratio of Tertiary Industry in GDP	2008	40.1	32-58	1820 1870
Ratio of Employment in the Secondary Industry	2007	32.4	32	1900

Source: 1. Data of China are from *Chinese Statistics Book 2008* and *Chinese National Economy and Social Development Statistic Report 2008*; 2. Ratio for Secondary/ Tertiary Industry of GDP, employment in the Secondary/Tertiary Industry of the United States are from *Chinese Modernization Report 2005*.

We also see that China's urbanization rate in 2007 and 2008 is 44.94% and 45.7%[1] respectively in the intermediate phase of urbanization, displaying a tremendous demand potential in the future. If the urban population grows up to two thirds of the total population from the 450 million currently to 900 million and the share of the tertiary industry in GDP to 50%, we can release the domestic demand for a long run for the economic growth. In fact, China is now accelerating the process of urbanization. We have every reason to believe that the future demand of Chinese market will be extremely vast.

4.2. An Ideal Investment Location

China's GDP per capita is only US $ 3,000, a level of the intermediate-level countries, with huge space for further promotion. China's abundant human capital and natural resources and vast areas are all advantages for attracting investments. We will discuss this by the following two points.

First, China is in the intermediate phase of industrialization, needing large amount of investment. Here is why. China's industrialization is in line with the U.S. intermediate phase of industrialization. According to our research, We select four indicators to describe the industrialization degree and economic development phase (See Table 2).

[1] Data of 2007 are from *Chinese Statistic Book 2008*, data of 2008 are from *Chinese National Economic and Social Development Report 2008*.

According to Table 2 and Categories of U.S economic development phrases[2], we can see that the share of the secondary industry in GDP in China is in line with the period 1950-1960 of U.S. which is the U.S. post-industrialization phase, while the ratio of employment in China corresponds to that of the year 1900 of U.S. which is the U.S. primary phase of industrialization. Hence, we can infer that the current economic development in China is in the intermediate period of industrialization.

For a big country with 1.3 billion people but the industrialization remaining in the intermediate phase, to complete the industrialization process, saying, the gradual transition into latter industrialization, post industrialization and even the modern industrial society, China needs accelerations in upgrading the industrial structure, expanding investment, and promoting the industrialization level.

Secondly, the international investors are very concerned whether China has a sound economic system for their investments. Over 30 years of reform and opening-up, in the process of economic transformation, China's economic system is gradually becoming matured. Moreover, the factor market, government management system, and the reform of state-owned firms are all making progresses, providing institutional assurance for foreign investments.

4.3. A New Global Investor

In the future reform and opening-up, China is sure to make shifts from commodity exportation to capital exportation, from capital agglomeration to capital radiation strategy, from a trade-oriented nation to a capital-oriented power.

China's rapid economic development and growing comprehensive national power help Chinese firms prepared for the international investment expansion. China's GDP per capita has exceeded US $3,000, which is fundamental to the outward investment. Meanwhile, Chinese government encourages and supports the qualified firms of all-kind ownerships to make

[2] Categories of economic development phrases in U.S.: pre-1870: agricultural society; 1870-1910: primary phrase of industrialization; 1910-1940: intermediate phrase of industrialization, where, 1910-1920 is the period for making shifts from the primary phrase of industrialization to the intermediate phrase; 1940-1970 is the latter period of industrialization; 1970-1992: post-industrialization; since 1992: modern society. Source: Li Xiaoxi, et al. *Research on China's Economy Development Phrases and Relevant Strategies*. Academic Journal of the Central University of Finance and Economics, 2007 (3).

overseas direct investments (ODI) or multinational operation, actively involving in economic globalization as well as the integration of world economy. Since 2009, the policies encouraging outward investments are released successively: *The Administrative Rules Governing Foreign Investment* by the Department of Commerce aims to encourage the cross-border investments or mergers and acquisitions. *The Foreign Exchange Regulations Concerning the Overseas Investment by Domestic Organizations* issued by the State Administration of Foreign Exchange tends to replace the approval by registration system for the administration of the overseas foreign exchange of the investment by domestic firms. Thereafter, the Department of Commerce declared that based on *The Administrative Regulations on Contracting Foreign Projects* of 2008, *The Administrative Regulation on Foreign Labor Cooperation* and *The Administrative Regulation on Foreign Investment Cooperation* will be introduced soon. In addition, to protect the rights and interests of Chinese firms in overseas investment, China has established bilateral mechanisms for economic and trade committee with more than 100 countries and regions all over the world and signed 127 bilateral investment protection agreements. The introduction of these policies and regulations will provide an all-round administrative assurance for Chinese overseas investment.

Based on the wealth accumulated from the rapid economic growth and the policies in favor of ODI, Chinese firms and households have started making large-scale international investment, which is growing rapidly (See Figure 4).

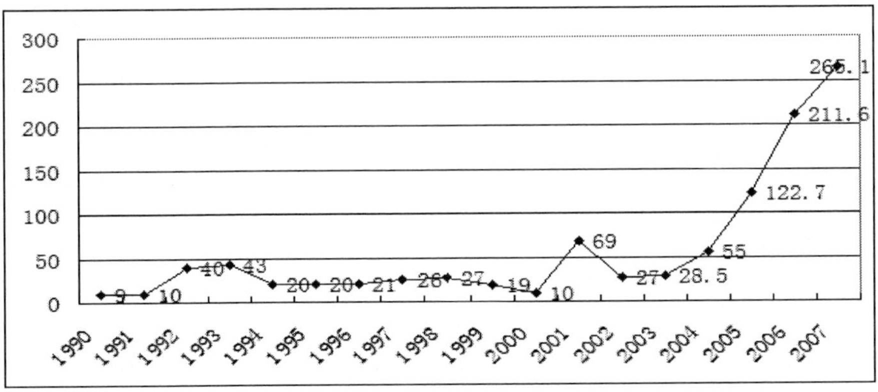

Source: Report of China's Overseas Direct Investment 2007, website of the Department of Commerce of China.

Figure 4. China's ODI Volume, 1990-2007 (Unit: US$ 100 million).

As the above figure shows, the China's ODI hits US $26.51 billion in 2007, up by 25.3% year on year. Moreover, the volume has been increasing greatly since 2002. From 2002 to 2007, the non-financial ODI has increased by 56% per annum.

Over the last year, due to the heavy hit of the global financial crisis, the real economy all over the world has sunk into deep recession. While foreign investors are laggard to invest in China, China's overseas investment becomes the highlight of the global economy. China's non-financial overseas investments in 2008 hit US$ 40.7 billion, up by 63.6%[3] year on year. In the second quarter of 2009, the overseas investment from China mainland (excluding Hong Kong and Macao) is US $10.8 billion (US$ 3.9 billion in the first quarter), up by 17%[4].

4.4. A Builder of New International Financial System

China advocates and participates actively in the reform of international financial system and in the optimization of the global financial supervision, striving for a new international financial order.

There are reasons for the reform of international financial system: (1) It does not reflect the changes in the economic powers in the world. Particularly, it does not enhance the share of developing economies in the international financial organizations, such as the discourse right for the emerging markets. (2) It lacks the supervision over the risk of cross- national finance, the arrangement of prewarning institutions, and effective supervision on the disordered flow of short-term capital.

Early at the G20 summit in 2008, China has made a series of suggestions and policy proposals on reforming current international currency and finance system, maintaining international financial stabilization, facilitating economic and financial policy coordination across the world, enhancing international currency and financial cooperation, and so on. The propositions have attracted much attention and been valued worldwide. Early in 2009, Zhou Xiaochuan, President of the People's Bank of China, had a detailed proposition that the

---

3 Source: *Statistical Communiqué of the People's Republic of China on the National Economic and Social Development 2008.*

4 Liu Zhendong, Zhang Xiaofang. *Australia Becomes the First Choice for Chinese Overseas Merger and acquisition*. Economic Information Daily, July 28, 2009.

international financial system should be reformed, including creating a type of international reserve currency depegged from sovereign countries and remaining stable for a long-run, to avoid the inherent defect of the sovereign credit currency as the reserve currency. He also proposed that IMF centrally manage some reserves for the member countries[5].

Overall, as a typical emerging market, China has been and will be more and more important in promoting the reform on international financial system and optimizing the global financial supervision.

[5] Zhou Xiaochuan. *Thoughts on Reform of International Currency System*. March 24, 2009. The official website of the People's Bank of China.

REFERENCES

Chen Jiagui, *China's Economic Prospect: Report of Spring,* Social Science Literature Press, Beijing, April, 2009.

Department of Commerce, *National Export Strategy: the second annual report of the Trade Promotion Coordinating Committee*, 2004.

Goldman Sachs, Global Economics Paper No.99, *Dreaming with BRICs: The Path to 2050*, Oct.1, 2003.

Goldman Sachs, Global Economics Paper No: 153, *The N-11: More Than an Acronym*, March, 2007.

IMF. World Economic Outlook Database. April, 2009.

Institute of Economic and Resources Management of Beijing Normal University, *A Report on the Development of China's Market Economy 2003*, China International Commerce and Trade Press, 2003.

Institute of Economic and Resources Management of Beijing Normal University, *A Report on the Development of China's Market Economy 2008*, Beijing Normal University Publishing House, 2008.

Li Xiaoxi. *China: A New Development Concept*. Chinese Economy Publishing House, 2008.

Li Xiaoxi, et al. *Discussion and Progress of Significant Theory Problems During the 30 Years of China's Reform and Opening-up*[J]. Finance and Trade Economics, 2008(11).

Edited by Li Xiaoxi, *Volume of China Economy Marketization* [M], Chongqing University Press, 2008.

Li Xiaoxi, et al. Evaluation on China' s Monetary and Financial Policies, Beijing: Renmin Publishing House, 2007.

Li Xiaoxi, et al. *Research on China's Economy Development Phrases and Relevant Strategies* [J]. Academic Journal of the Central University of Finance and Economics, 2007, (3).

Liu Zhendong, Zhang Xiaofang, *Australia has become the first-choice for Chinese overseas merger and acquisition,* Economic Information Daily, July 28th, 2009.

National Bureau of Statistics. *China Monthly Economic Indicators* [J], 2009 (2).

National Economic and Social Development Statistical Communiquй of every calendar year.

National Statistical Yearbook of every calendar year.

Rao Huilin, *Urban Economics (Volume I)* [M], Northeast University of Finance and Economics Press, August 1999.

Shang Jun, Fu Yunwei, *Emerging markets step onto historical front on response to financial crisis*, Economic Information Daily, Sep. 16th, 2009

Survey and Statistics Department of the People's Bank of China, *Central Bank Macroeconomic Situation Analysis Report of the Second Quarter of 2009*, July 28th, 2009.

Wang Jian, *Population Urbanization is the strategy direction for expending domestic demand* [N], China Economic Herald, April 18th, 2009.

Zhang Rongnan, Time for investment overseas [N], China Daily, June 22nd, 2009.

INDEX

I

J

L

M

N

O

P

U

V

W